my itty-bitty bio

Cristiano Ronaldo

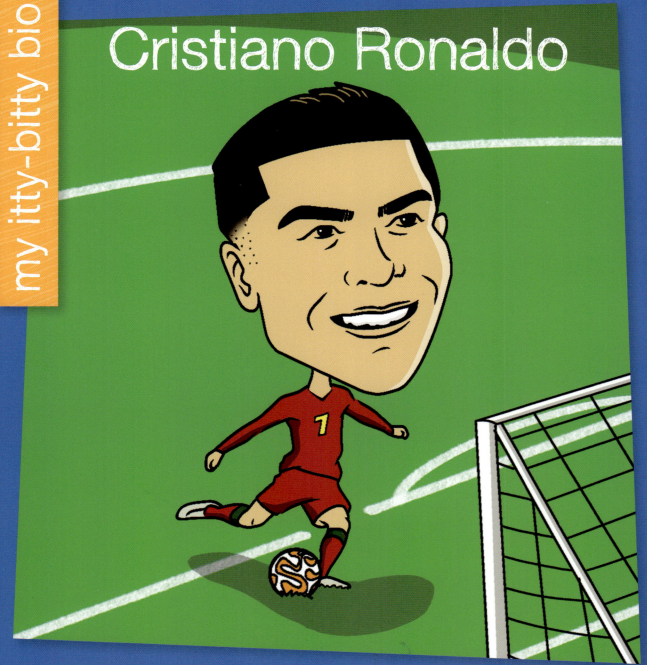

Published in the United States of America by Cherry Lake Publishing
Ann Arbor, Michigan
www.cherrylakepublishing.com

Reading Adviser: Beth Walker Gambro, MS, Ed., Reading Consultant, Yorkville, IL
Illustrator: Leo Trinidad

Photo Credits: © proslgn/Shutterstock, 5; © Koonsiri Boonnak/Dreamstime.com, 7; © Allstar Picture Library Ltd/Alamy Stock Photo, 9, 22; © Vlad1988/Shutterstock, 11; © Marcos Mesa Sam Wordley/Shutterstock, 13; © NurPhoto SRL/Alamy Stock Photo, 15, 23; © PA Images/Alamy Stock Photo, 17; © Aflo Co. Ltd./Alamy Stock Photo, 19; © Maciej Rogowski Photo/Shutterstock, 21

Copyright © 2026 by Cherry Lake Publishing
All rights reserved. No part of this book may be reproduced or utilized in any form or by any means without written permission from the publisher.

Cherry Lake Press is an imprint of Cherry Lake Publishing Group

Library of Congress Cataloging-in-Publication Data has been filed and is available at catalog.loc.gov.

Printed in the United States of America

table of contents

My Story 4

Timeline .22

Glossary 24

Index 24

About the author: When not writing, Dr. Virginia Loh-Hagan serves as the Executive Director for AANAPISI Affairs and the APIDA Center at San Diego State University. She is also the Co-Executive Director of The Asian American Education Project. She lives in San Diego with her very tall husband and very naughty dogs.

About the illustrator: Leo Trinidad is a *New York Times* bestselling comic book artist, illustrator, and animator from Costa Rica. For more than 12 years, he's been creating content for children's books and TV shows. Leo created the first animated series ever produced in Central America and founded Rocket Cartoons, one of the most successful animation studios in Latin America. He is also the 2018 winner of the Central American Graphic Novel contest.

my story

I was born in 1985. I was born in Portugal.

I can speak four languages.

My father worked at a local soccer club. He managed the **equipment**.

He introduced me to soccer.

I played at a young age.
I played **professional** soccer.

I was still a teen.

Do you like to play soccer?

I am fast. I am strong. I am skilled. I take risks. I work hard.

I train all the time.

I won many games. I won many awards.

I am one of the best soccer players ever.

I have broken many records.

I'm the top scorer.

I love my fans. I have many fans on **social media**. I share personal moments.

I make connections.

Are you a fan? Who are your heroes?

I help others. I donate money. I support **causes**.

I donate blood.

My legacy lives on.

I am a star on and off the soccer field.

What would you like to ask me?

timeline

2003

1970

Born
1985

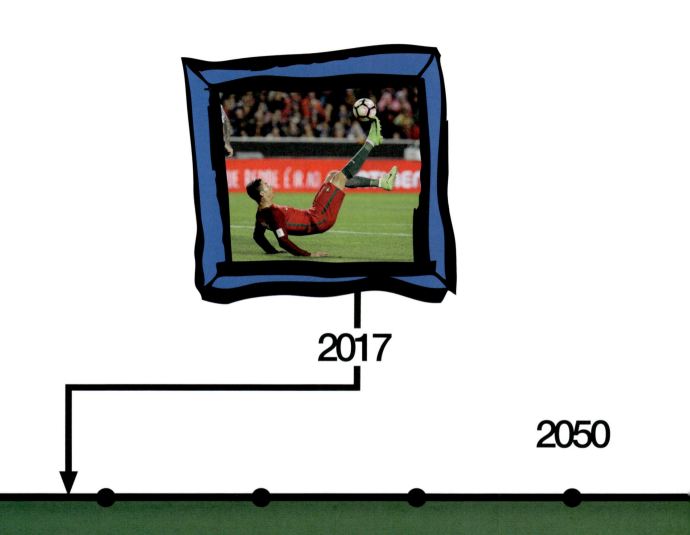

2017

2050

glossary

causes (KAWZ-uhz) activities that support others in need

equipment (ih-KWIP-muhnt) items or gear needed to do something, such as play a sport

professional (pruh-FESH-nuhl) related to a job; describing when someone is paid for their work

social media (SOH-shuhl MEE-dee-uh) websites and apps where people can create and share content

index

birth, 4, 22

causes, 18

family, 6
fans, 16–17

Portugal, 4–5
professional career, 8–17, 22–23

soccer, 6–21
social media, 16

talent, 4, 8, 10, 12, 14, 20
timeline, 22–23